The World of Internet Marketing
The Basics

Jonathan Edward Goodman

ISBN: 1482074532
ISBN-13: 978-1482074536

FOR DUC

CONTENTS

ACKNOWLEDGMENTS

Throughout my career I have been incredibly fortunate to have found guidance in those around me both in and out of the workplace.

Danny Dover along with James and Arlene Martell formed my industry cheerleading squad.

A special thank you to Mike Gruhn for all the awesome cartoons that precede each chapter.

Finally, My family means everything to me and I thank them for their support.

INTRODUCTION

When I was a kid there was a coffee mug sold in a shop near my home. On the mug was a cow in sunglasses holding a balloon surrounded by waist high grass. The phrase on the mug read "Outstanding in the Field". I thought this was hysterical. I love double entendre and this to me was the height of perfection.

Now, as an adult, in some way that cow has come to symbolize my career. On one hand, I understand Internet marketing. I've been in the field for over twenty years. I've worked for some great companies and gained a ton of experience.

On the other hand, I sometimes feel like I'm shouting into the wind. I think it's very difficult gaining a voice in this or any industry. Marketing of the self is everything now. I love social media. It allows you to reacquaint yourself with old friends and find like-minded new ones. Businesses can utilize social media to build a client base and increase sales.

The only issue I have is that the rules of engagement dictate that the person spending the most amount of time on it wins. But is that who you really want to follow? What are they doing that they have that much time? As a client, if they're so busy marketing themselves can they really successfully market you?

Someone once said to me that there are two things you must do in order to get noticed in this industry. The first is to speak at as many conferences as possible. Ok, that's fairly easy. All I need to do is put together speaking proposals. Goodness knows there's a search conference going on somewhere in the world nearly every day.

But again, I had to ask myself, do I want to jet set around promoting myself or did I want to do the best I could for my clients. I chose to limit the number of conferences to a couple a year and exclusively stay on the East Coast.

The second thing this person suggested I do in order to get noticed was write a book. Which as I found out through this exercise, is a lot harder than it looks. The original plan was to write ten chapters on everything from website design to advanced search engine optimization. It was going to be an A to Z manifesto of my observations and knowledge of the industry.

What I found, as I started writing, was that each chapter was getting longer and longer; filled with additional topics beyond the original outline. So for the sake of both my sanity and the fear that this book would never see the light of day, I decided to split the book into three volumes. You are holding the first volume, which is all about the basics.

It's written for the novice small business owner who needs to understand how to market to an online audience. It's also meant to protect you against unscrupulous and sometimes unknowledgeable companies trying to sell their services within this industry. I don't blame them entirely. There is a lot of information out there and some of it is just incorrect. Internet marketing is one part art, one part science and a very good mix of skill. I feel it's very similar to the tattoo industry. Anyone can call themselves a tattoo artist but there's a significant difference between skill and junk. And when it's on your arm or on your website, you want the skilled professional not the fly-by-night guy.

Thank you for purchasing this book. I hope you enjoy it. I sincerely appreciate it. And be on the lookout for the next volume coming soon.

Jonathan Edward Goodman

ONLINE BRAND MANAGEMENT

I n the early 1930's Harvard graduate Neil McElroy joined Proctor & Gamble and quickly concluded that the organization of the advertising departments were counterintuitive to the needs of the product. He wrote a three page memo laying out his vision of change. He believed that in order to compete with a diversifying market, the position of brand manager needed to be created so each one could immerse themselves in the study of a single product line.

The concept of branding has been around since the ancient Egyptians with the branding of farm animals in order to avoid theft. By the 13th century English bakers were required by law to brand each product they sold. It wasn't until the early 19th century that branding became a way to promote a company's level of expertise. Watching the Antiques Roadshow you'll notice how the experts use the branding of an item to determine its authenticity.

Today, the Internet is what is driving brand management. A major benefit of online brand management is the ability to publish information that isn't limited by geography or time. Now the brand manager can focus on a niche audience with specific behavior and segment content according to behavioral targets like age, gender, and geography. The brand manager can also choose what the niche will see for advertising.

A company like Toyota can setup an advertising campaign for a niche audience of people searching for keyword terms relevant to shopping for a new vehicle. They can segment the campaign to show trucks to searchers geographically located in the Midwest while showing fuel efficient hybrids to others geographically located in the North West.

This is called geo-targeting and it allows the brand manager to deliver different content to people based on state, city, zip code, or other criteria. All of this segmentation lowers the cost of advertising and improves return on investment; allowing localized small businesses to compete against multi-national corporations.

The brand manager controls the image of the brand and tries to connect the emotional feelings of the consumer with that product or company. The strength of a brand is determined by the company's ability to build an emotional response with its clients. One of the best ways to monitor your brand is to setup a Google Alerts. All businesses large and small should create alerts based on the name of their company as well as all executive staff. You can choose to get the alerts once a day, once a week, or as it happens.

Today, everything is a brand - including you the individual. We've gone from corporate brand recognition of companies like Quaker Oats, Campbells Soup, and Coca-Cola to individual brands of Kim Kardashian, Martha Stewart and Oprah Winfrey. These women have millions of social media followers, visitors to their websites, and product tie-ins that reinforce their individual brand. When they have something to say, it's heard by the masses.

In fact when we compare these corporate brands to their personal brand counterparts we find a staggering lack of traction from corporations in social media. In the **Corporate Brands on Twitter** chart, shown on the following page, we see that @Quaker has 23K followers, @CampbellSoupCo has 10K followers, and @CocaColaCo has 56K followers.

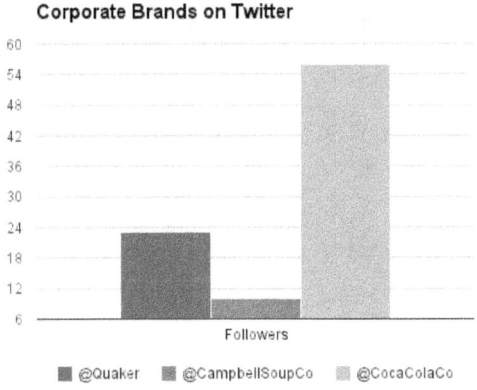

Comparing that to the **Personal Brands on Twitter** chart, found below, we find that @KimKardashian has 16 Million followers, @MarthaStewart has 2 Million followers, and @Oprah has 15 Million followers. The celebrity individual brand is stronger and reaches a larger audience than corporate brands that have been around for several decades.

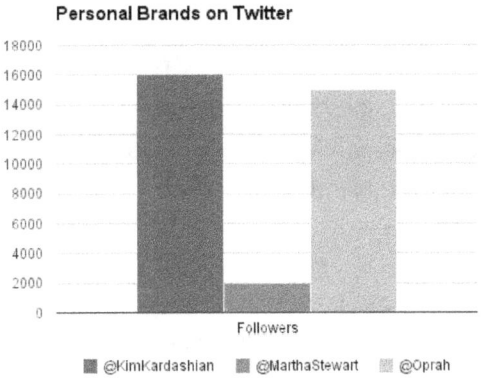

This shift has less to do with our obsession of celebrities and more to do with the disconnect we have with large corporations. Despite the Supreme Court's ruling that a corporation is a person; we as humans have a hard time relating to a multinational conglomerate. We follow human celebrities because we connect with them on a personal level. This simply doesn't happen with products we consume.

Is it possible to build a personal brand despite not being a celebrity? Can you create enough momentum where your name translates to sales of a product?

The first step to building your online identity is having a blog. Everyone and every company needs a blog. It tells people who you are and what your company is about. It allows you to grow an audience and become an authority on a subject. In a sea of voices shouting about their business, the blog allows you to be heard.

According to a Blogging.org survey conducted in 2012, it is estimated there are 31 million bloggers in the United States with 500,000 new blog posts every day. Over 25 million blog pages are viewed every month and 60% of US businesses have a blog but unfortunately 65% of those haven't updated it within a year or more.

The search engines wants to see new content. It is the difference between top ranking and obscurity. If you aren't willing or able to provide new content on a semi-regular basis the game is already lost.

Gaining Credibility

There are three goals you need to focus on when building out your blog. Get the site ranked in the search engines; increase traffic to your website; and convert visitors into sales. That's it! It's not rocket science...it's not brain surgery.

Google is the place everyone goes to in order to find the information they need. As much as Bing and Yahoo would like you to believe they matter they simply don't. There are some estimates that put Google at 88% of market share for search. They are the definitive authority in determining what the searcher sees.

The first goal of your blog is to provide original authoritative content that Google will recognize and rank thereby placing it on the first page of a regularly searched keyword. A well ranked website tells the search community that you are trusted by Google. That trust will lead into the second goal of increased traffic to your website. Then once they are on your site it's completely dependent on you to convert them into a sale.

So how do you build an authoritative site that Google will want to rank? It's easy to hide behind a website and provide fake or flawed information. Consumers take a long hard look before trusting anyone online. With the exception of Manti Te'o's girlfriend.

There are several ways to build online credibility for yourself, your blog, and your company's website. The most important is to share personal information about yourself. Share photos and stories about events you attended. I'm not talking about your night out to the Justin Bieber concert but instead keep it relevant to your industry. Include photos from conferences and stories about interesting sessions. Be real and show your flaws. If you've made wild predictions about your industry that were completely wrong, own up to it. Only promote high-quality external products and links. If you're not a doctor don't advocate for Viagra. Encourage people to contact you directly with their questions. Make your website contact form easily accessible and make sure to respond to legitimate questions in a timely manner.

In May, 2011 Amit Singhal wrote a post on the Google Webmaster Central Blog that outlined 23 questions that Google uses to determine if a website or blog is of high-quality.

1. Would you trust the information presented in this article?

2. Is this article written by an expert or enthusiast who knows the topic well, or is it more shallow in nature?

3. Does the site have duplicate, overlapping, or redundant articles on the same or similar topics with slightly different keyword variations?

4. Would you be comfortable giving your credit card information to this site?

5. Does this article have spelling, stylistic, or factual errors?

6. Are the topics driven by genuine interests of readers of the site, or does the site generate content by attempting to guess what might rank well in search engines?

7. Does the article provide original content or information, original reporting, original research, or original analysis?

8. Does the page provide substantial value when compared to other pages in search results?

9. How much quality control is done on content?

10. Does the article describe both sides of a story?

11. Is the site a recognized authority on its topic?

12. Is the content mass-produced by or outsourced to a large number of creators, or spread across a large network of sites, so that individual pages or sites don't get as much attention or care?

13. Was the article edited well, or does it appear sloppy or hastily produced?

14. For a health related query, would you trust information from this site?

15. Would you recognize this site as an authoritative source when mentioned by name?

16. Does this article provide a complete or comprehensive description of the topic?

17. Does this article contain insightful analysis or interesting information that is beyond obvious?

18. Is this the sort of page you'd want to bookmark, share with a

friend, or recommend?

19. Does this article have an excessive amount of ads that distract from or interfere with the main content?

20. Would you expect to see this article in a printed magazine, encyclopedia or book?

21. Are the articles short, unsubstantial, or otherwise lacking in helpful specifics?

22. Are the pages produced with great care and attention to detail vs. less attention to detail?

23. Would users complain when they see pages from this site?

From these questions you can gather that Google is trying to determine if you have knowledge of your professed industry and if you are adding value to your field.

Asking random people these 23 questions will provide you with an unbiased view of your site. You can use a company like Survey Monkey or Amazon's Mechanical Turk, which allows you to hire people to do simple tasks like take a survey.

Recently, I've added four additional questions when creating these surveys for my clients:

1. Is the article focused on current topics of conversation within the industry?

2. Does the author write frequently?

3. Does the author come off as unreasonable, bitter, condemning, crude, paranoid, racist, sexist, or vulgar?

4. Does the author tolerate opposing points of view?

In building up your credibility you don't want to give the visitor the impression they are only there to click on an advertisement. So I always recommend never using pop-up ads on your website.

It's also important to monitor your comments and watch for spam. In fact I often tell my clients that until they've reached critical mass they should disable comments. I've seen too often a competitor leave a nasty message and the author responds with an additionally nasty quip. It soon becomes a long drawn out confrontation for everyone to read.

Understand that credibility doesn't happen overnight. Sometimes it doesn't happen at all. Only you can determine how much effort you are going to put into blogging but at the end of the day if the result is to increase clients or sales you need to stick with it.

Listen Up

When I started in this industry over twenty years ago optimization was about HTML coding. Honestly, it was a bunch of stuff you're not supposed to do anymore: keyword stuffing, cloaking, hidden text, etc. Then the focus shifted and was more about meta data and backlinks. Now optimization is all about content. I've gone from a computer science geek to an English major nerd.

Search engines want important content to be found. A search should provide the best, most relevant, useful, and up-to-date information available to the searcher. Optimization work serves to enhance already good content and increase its likelihood of being found.

So if you're scratching your head without a clue about what to write, believe me I've been there. Coming up with ideas for blog posts is difficult. Especially if you're trying to gain an audience and write nearly every day. A lot of people get stuck because they don't know what to put in a blog. They look at their computer screen and ask 'what will people be interested in reading'. Instead they should be looking in the mirror and asking what it is they want to talk about.

As funny as it might sound the Kevin Costner movie Field of Dreams said it perfectly "Build it and they will come". If you talk about what you want to talk about you'll be able to write every day of the week.

Ask yourself what is your objective in writing a blog? A great starting point is to listen to your customers. Ask your employees what kind of questions they get from clients. Answer each of those questions in detail within a blog post. Then when a potential customer comes to your site and reads through your articles some of their questions will already be answered.

Write about things that interest you and your target audience. You have to start with thinking like a customer. When you sit down with a client, listen to the questions they ask. These questions can become the titles and topics for your blog posts where you can tell everyone what they need to know.

If you want to establish your company as the authority on a product or service in your industry, you have to be the one answering the questions that consumers ask. That way, they'll come to you for help and advice.

It's also critical to listen to what industry leaders are talking about. These leaders didn't wake up one morning and everyone was following them. Some industry leaders have great public relations and marketing skills with dynamic personalities. Others dedicate long arduous hours to producing great material that needs to be heard. Both have value within an industry. Just make sure when you start following someone that you're focused on the message and not the performance.

Start by listening to everyone talking in your industry. You'll naturally gravitate toward people you like, people you believe in, and people who are telling the truth. There are a lot of people talking hogwash in every industry. Everyone wants to be heard but some just ride on their arrogance and not their intellect. You'll find it's easy sifting through the jumbled double talkers to the real intellects with the knowledge.

The Taboo Talk About Price

The Internet is the place to get all your questions answered. Nothing is taboo on the Internet. Well actually, there is still one big taboo: Talking about price. Only a small percentage of websites, around 1-2%, talk price. Hiding your price isn't going to help you win customers or beat out the competition. Your competition already knows your pricing and if they don't they weren't really your competition to start.

So, instead of hiding it, make it a point of discussion in your blog articles. Put the power in your hands. Take the sticker shock out of your client presentations. Anyone interested in working with you is going to do their homework before picking up the phone. If they see an article mentioning price they'll know if they can play ball.

If you've ever gone into a sales meeting with a well written proposal only to find that the executive immediately flips to the cost page and then disregards the content of the document; you understand the need for prior price disclosure. If that executive knew what your costs were before sitting down, their focus would be on the details of the presentation and they would be listening specifically to how you differ from the next guy.

You're thinking that prior price disclosure is going to prevent you from getting in the door. But isn't that really what you want? Would you rather waste your time trying to convince a company to do business with you or spend your time talking to a company that already knows they want to bring you on as a vendor?

Hiding behind the curtain didn't work for the Great and Powerful Oz and it's not going to work for you. If you hem and haw when someone asks you about pricing it's going to make you seem weak and insecure. Would you walk into a car dealership where all the prices of the vehicles were hidden?

It's true that some of your competitors are going to see it as an opportunity to undercut your pricing. Working in the optimization industry, I've seen pricing all over the place. From less than a $100 to over $2K a month. I meet people every day that complain about getting tons of phone calls trying to sell them on optimization. Each vendor undercutting the price of the last call. Remove yourself from the race to the bottom by providing clear intelligent information with supportive evidence for your pricing.

Every industry has bottom feeders and you have to choose if you're going to play in that game. In the legal profession there are lawyers providing free consultations. There are eye doctors and dentists giving out coupons. Are you going to get eye surgery from the best or cheapest doctor? Should people be hiring you because you're cheap or because you're good at what you do?

Worse than being the bottom feeder is the level of clientele you'll attract. If your prices are too low you'll end up spinning your wheels working for pennies. It's a strange world but people who pay the least complain the most. You don't have time for that. If you are honest about your prices in your blog the bottom feeder will simply go away.

Jonathan Edward Goodman

Jonathan Edward Goodman

MASTERING LINKEDIN MARKETING

I n my opinion LinkedIn, a social network for professionals, is terribly underutilized. The site launched in 2003 and despite having over 175 million active users; nearly half of all members spend less than two hours a week on the site.

The problem for LinkedIn is that most people don't see it as a social marketing tool like Facebook and Twitter. While their member numbers are lower than Facebook, they are higher than Twitter and Google+. But it's truly an excellent website for clients and potential clients to connect on a personal level.

Here are some additional important facts about LinkedIn:

- Over 90% of LinkedIn members are using the free unpaid version.

- 20% of members have between 100 and 200 first degree connections. I personally have over 500.

- Only 50% of members have 100% completed profiles.

- 71% of all Americans with at least a four-year degree are on LinkedIn.

- The majority of users are only using LinkedIn to research people and companies.

The misconception about LinkedIn is it's a site for people looking for work. In fact the site is setup to be a fantastic tool for small businesses looking to network with new clients.

LinkedIn has a powerful email selection tool for alerts on saved searches, custom news, comments, and group discussions. Due to the sites popularity, email messages from people trying to contact you don't get caught in spam filters.

There are two great ways to improve your network on LinkedIn. First, through mutual connections. All of your contacts have their own connections, which to you are second degree contacts. You can ask your contacts to make introductions to these secondary connections on your behalf. You can even go one step further to a third degree, whereby your contact has a connection with a contact you'd like to meet. It's a little difficult getting everyone on board to grant you access but if it's a big name contact it might be worth it.

The second and far more powerful way to improve your network is through LinkedIn Groups. LinkedIn has nearly three million groups and while many are employment related, a fair number of them cover professional and career issues as well as academic and corporate alumni. Over 80% of LinkedIn members belong to a group but only about half of them actively participate. Groups can be private, members only or open to all Internet users. Unfortunately, the level of openness will also determine the level of spam. Groups that are open to all Internet users tend to contain more spam than those that are private or members only. Groups that don't have a good moderator will also find themselves having to sift through spam and when a group is both open to all users and is poorly moderated - watch out cause it's going to be spam city.

LinkedIn Groups are great for connecting like-minded people together. It is also great for finding potential customer hang outs. For example, an ecommerce company shouldn't just be in groups about the business of ecommerce. Instead they should find a group of enthusiast for the products they sell.

Though the majority of users are involved with less than 10 groups at a time. If you're looking to slim down the number of groups you're involved with start by removing those that have a limited number of followers. Unless these small numbered groups are seriously dedicated to a niche and actively participating they really aren't going to provide you the networking benefits you want. It's important to continuously remind members of these groups that you are there. The more you're in front of potential customers the more likely they are to pay attention. A weekly or bi-weekly message will help you stay relevant. Otherwise you'll be lost in the chatter. Look to provide answers to questions as well as providing your opinion on group discussions or even message the group with an industry relevant article.

Ultimately being the leader of a LinkedIn Group provides the most leads and the most opportunity to promote your website. You can put the website URL in the group profile, add it to the welcome message and even post it in group discussions. However, you don't want to bombard members to the point they feel the only reason you created the group was to promote your company's services.

Don't name the group after your company if you are looking to attract industry experts and enthusiasts and not just your employees. Make it more inviting by naming it something industry related but make sure to include important keywords so people can find you in the LinkedIn Group Search. LinkedIn recently made improvements to their search making it easier to find the group that's right for you.

LinkedIn even allows for the creation of sub-groups. If your group becomes large enough or geographically specific enough you can create sub-groups. In fact as the leader of the group you can suggest that geographic sub-groups create Meetups whereby people can get to know each other face-to-face in the real world.

When creating your LinkedIn Group start by inviting employees and current clients then go on to promote the group on your website and other social media outlets. Once you've gained enough members, so there is an easy flow of conversation, you can invite industry leaders who will be more willing to join if they see an active group. Industry leaders themselves have followers that will be interested in your group.

Be careful of people who join groups just to promote themselves. You don't want a member who isn't truly engaging with other members to take over the conversation. If they are just standing on a soapbox shouting about their product, you have the ability to kick them out.

Developing LinkedIn Brand Identity

There are several activities on LinkedIn that will help you develop your presence and establish your brand.

Build an Outstanding Profile - The information at the top of your profile is seen first so make sure it is complete and looks great to anyone checking out your page. LinkedIn has expanded the level of detailed information you can put in your profile. Some of the newly added sections like Projects, Honors & Awards, Organizations, Test Scores, and Courses lend themselves to recent college students or grads while sections like Languages, Patents, Certifications, and Publications help market the constant professional. I'm still hoping they add a lecturer or conference section for people like me who speak at industry events.

Focus on Connections - Don't limit the people you can connect with; it will limit your opportunities. Focus on growing your connections.

Post Frequently on LinkedIn - People who are active on the site often rank higher in LinkedIn searches. There is also a correlation between the frequency of posting and an increase in the number of followers they receive. Just make sure that your posts are relevant and informative; they should be rich in content. You should also post original comments and stay away from just retweeting others' messages.

Take Time to Comment - When you comment on someone's post or in a group, other people see that information. If it is helpful or informative it will allow them to see that you're knowledgeable. Use both your own blog and your presence on LinkedIn to help establish you as an authority in your industry.

Company Pages

Beyond the personal resume profile, LinkedIn allows you to create a company page. This is a great way to communicate with your business audience where you can reach potential clients, industry leaders, strategic allies and possible new employees. Company pages include images, product and service promotion, and links to your websites as well as your company's YouTube videos.

The product and services pages are so powerful you can even segment your audience so they see a different landing page based on criteria you define. You can segment by company size, job function, industry, seniority and even geography. Additionally, the company pages allow you to create multiple banners each linking back to specific pages on your website.

Recent improvements to the "People You May Know" section now allows you to segment by school or company. This makes it worthwhile to keep going back. You should try to take one hour every month to go through the "People You May Know" section and add relationships.

LinkedIn Influence

LinkedIn has a strong presence as a website and if you want to develop influence with your customers, you'll need to develop that presence. This will build on your success as you develop more content on the site. You must be seen as credible, visible on the site, engaged and resourceful for people who are interested in your industry, and accessible and generous with your time. This established presence will enhance your reputation as a person of authority in your business or industry.

LinkedIn also has a slightly ruthless side to it. Since the LinkedIn search allows for company segmentation you could research your competition and see who's on their team, what skills they have, and even go so far as to make introductions. It's your opportunity to try to steal someone away. Additionally, if your competition managed a group you could find out who they are connected to too. Often customers and partners of your competition will be associated with the group making it easy for you to make contact.

Recently, LinkedIn has been experimenting with a new interaction feature called INfluencers. LinkedIn is forming expert panels including Barack Obama, Richard Branson, and T. Boone Pickens to discuss and debate national issues. I respect LinkedIn's attempts to broaden and increase activity for its audience but it's hard enough for most people to see LinkedIn as anything more than a job board. My guess is that adding INfluencers isn't going to be as successful as they are hoping.

However, when LinkedIn opens the INfluencer program to include bloggers, entrepreneurs, and self-help gurus it could be a great addition to your social media strategy. You can fill out the INfluencer application to see if you qualify. http://partner.linkedin.com/influencer/

LinkedIn Service Provider Directory

Though little known and thus rarely used the LinkedIn Service Provider Directory allows you to promote your company within a massive 'yellow pages' style listing. After achieving six recommendations from your contacts LinkedIn will add you into this directory. Unfortunately, there is no ability for you to change or modify any of the listing details. Hopefully, LinkedIn will make an effort to add detailed interactivity. Otherwise this directory is as complicated for the searcher as it is for those listed.

LinkedIn Social Media

There are two important pieces of software relating to social media that need to be mentioned. The first is HootSuite. There is no greater service to manage your social network announcements. It allows you to create and monitor your Tweets, Facebook Posts, LinkedIn Announcements and Google+ messages. It's easy to use and allows for management of multiple user accounts. You can automate the scheduler or specify time and date in the calendar. In fact what I usually do is push everything through the automated system and then go back into the calendar to see when everything will launch. I then move things around to suite my needs and those of my clients.

The other important social media tool is the share buttons for all the major social media networks. It is critical that your blog have these share buttons. I'm not talking about the drop downs that confuse and enrage visitors. You only need four share buttons on your website: Twitter, Facebook, Google+, and LinkedIn.

Cool LinkedIn Tools

In recent years LinkedIn has provided a warm welcome to developers looking to improve the site using tools. Here are my top five favorite tools that integrate with LinkedIn:

Slideshare.net is a website unto itself but holds a great integration with LinkedIn. You can upload slide presentations on SlideShare and then push them through your LinkedIn profile so they show up on both sites.

CardMunch is a free iPhone app that transcribes photos of business cards and cross-references them with the owners LinkedIn profile making them a new connection.

LunchMeet is also a free iPhone app perfect for those looking to meet complete strangers. Your social skills have to be primed and your networking should be cranked up to 11 in order to participate in what most would find to be a nerve wracking social experiment. The purpose of LunchMeet is to "never eat alone" and that's exactly what you're going to do when you broadcast your available mealtime to complete strangers interested in having a meal with you.

InMaps is a fun cool tool that provides a visual representation of what your connection universe looks like. You can see from the representation of my connections that I have little pockets of people linked to me for very different reasons. Some of these connections are school alumni while others are previous employment. The exciting area are the connectors between the clusters. These people bridge the gap from one cluster to another and can help make the right connections.

Jonathan Goodman

Creative Portfolio Display is probably the most utilized enhancement for artists looking to display their portfolio on LinkedIn. It's both free and easy to use with unlimited upload capability for multimedia files.

Jonathan Edward Goodman

SOCIAL MEDIA MARKETING

S ocial media marketing is the creation and distribution of unique content through social networks made up of individuals with similar interests or professions. Those individuals receiving the marketing messages can in turn promote it to their social networks thereby growing the potential reach. Businesses with a social media strategy are able to establish themselves as an authority and increase brand awareness. Many companies use social media as a first line of defense for customer service issues and reputation management. While other businesses are using it for market research and product development.

Social media was born out of Web 2.0. A term originally coined by Tim O'Reilly and John Battelle in their opening remarks at the first Web 2.0 Conference back in 2004. As they saw it, the difference between Web 2.0 and everything that came before it was a development platform at the browser level not the desktop. Their prediction was that this radical change would allow customers to build businesses for you. This is something we see rampant every day with user-generated content sites like Facebook and Twitter.

In the marketing world, Web 2.0 offered the ability to uniquely engage with the consumer on product development, service enhancements, and promotions. Companies could build out wikis and social networks along with producing podcasts and micro blogs for niche audiences.

Blogging is an important part of your social media marketing strategy. In 2012 Blogging.org conducted a survey of a thousand bloggers. The compiled data showed certain commonalities between the majority of bloggers.

Most use the WordPress software to write their blogs. WordPress is the number one open source content management software on the planet. However, while some companies have utilized WordPress to create full websites the software still suffers from a stigma mistakenly marking it exclusively for blogging. It is true that WordPress started out as a blogging tool but it has become a full software package able to handle the most robust website requirements.

Blogging.org estimates there are over 40 Million blogs and company websites currently using WordPress. They believe there are nearly 500K new posts per day with 400K daily comments. They also suggest over 300 Million people view content that originated from a blog each day and that 25 Billion pages are viewed each month.

The survey also found that 60% of companies with an online presence have a blog but that only 35% of those update with new content at least once a month. The other 65% barely update blog content within a year.

If blogging is part of your strategy, it's critical you understand how it works, why it works, and what you need to do to make it successful. Blogging can be used to promote your business, your hobbies and yourself. Self-promotion is the key to successful blogging. In fact if you folded your business promotion into your self-promotion you'll be ten times more successful. Why is that? It's simple. People want to connect with other people. This holds true for the marketing of your business too.

Let's say for example you're an accountant. As a person, I like my accountant a lot. As a career, I yawn even saying the word "accountant". My accountant comes to me and says he's starting a blog...another big yawn. I'm not interested in reading an accounting blog. In fact no one outside of the accounting industry is going to read an accounting blog. So my advice to my accountant is not to write about accounting but instead write about himself.

Have you ever given a pet a pill? Now, they have these little pocket pills, which work great but years ago you had to try everything from rolled up pieces of bread to a spoonful of peanut butter and your pet would often times just eat around the pill and spit it out.

It's the same analogy to writing a business blog. Write about you and softly wrap relevant concepts related to industry keywords inside. More people will read stories about your life including an aspect of your business then read a lecture on a topic they have no interest in.

Guest Blogging

Blogging done the right way can help promote your company. But there are steps you can take to further promote your blog thereby promoting yourself and your business. Building your own blog can oftentimes be an isolating experience. It requires you sitting by your computer filling pages and pages of content with your thoughts. Many bloggers take up semi-permanent residency at a local coffee house just to get away from the numbing quiet of their own home.

If you're running a business you'll most likely have some kind of office space. The downside to that is you're going to be pulled away at a moment's notice for a more important task and ultimately you'll find yourself right back in your home writing the content needed for your blog to succeed.

However, once you've established yourself and have gained a small audience you can reach out to other popular bloggers and ask to guest post on their site. It will help you increase your brand, develop a larger audience, draw on positive sentiment, and leverage the power of your influence. The exposure you can gain from just one blog post placed on the right website can be the difference between a couple of people visiting your site to tens of thousands.

Approaching another blogger can sometimes be a daunting task. All the bloggers I have ever dealt with were at least hospitable but many of them simply didn't understand the power of guest blogging. It's important when choosing the blogger you're going to approach that you look for someone with a complementary blog to your own. Finding a blogger who fits your needs can take time. Look for someone already talking about your industry. That blogger's audience will be far more interested in what you have to offer.

Remember, a well-placed guest blog can help you find new audience members and ultimately additional customers. The popular blogger already has a fan base. Many of which are relying on the blogger to guide them in matters of importance. Since they already trust the blogger, they automatically trust those that guest post for them. It's like an instant endorsement. Just keep in mind that it might take several blog posts on the popular bloggers website before you reach the maximum audience available.

Also, understand what the ultimate goal is. If it's to gain more clients than steer clear of blogs whining about debt. In fact it's good advice to stay away from any blog with a negative slant. While sarcasm is an effective writing tool you don't want the blogger to constantly drag down the reader or belittle them.

The audience, the increase in visitors, the exposure are all great; but it doesn't compare to the added SEO you gain by backlinking content within the blog post to your website. If your guest post is on a popular website with lots of traffic and they've established their brand with the search engines; you in turn will be gaining a much needed backlink from that site. The opportunity is yours but you need to know how to take advantage of it. Make sure the backlink is coming from anchor text with a specific keyword you are trying to gain ranking. Anchor text is the word or phrase that appears to the user as a clickable hyperlink and in doing so serves to define the content behind the link it represents.

Where to Find Blogs to Guest Post

When you're a big brand it's easy to find popular bloggers to talk about your product. In fact many large size companies have advertising dollars that go directly to promoting through bloggers.

It's a harder challenge for small and localized businesses to make those contacts. Often times they don't have the budget or the brand to entice popular bloggers. That's why small brands need to focus on areas beyond money. Instead you should be willing to provide interviews with your staff and give away product samples or send them a free invitation to a conference or concert.

Have you ever heard the phrase "Gratitude will get you everywhere"? Being nice is the best approach. Be professional and treat these bloggers with the respect you'd give to journalists. Focus on building a long-term relationship that you can strengthen over time. Brand yourself as an authority on a specific subject and let the blogger know they can utilize you at any point if they have questions.

Your advice and expertise are invaluable and the best thing is it's free. A popular blogger doesn't continually want to quote the same person over and over. After a while they will look like they don't have any other resources. Remind the blogger of your value by occasionally sending them your quotes on different issues that they write about. If the relationship is growing, the blogger will eventually trust you enough to use one of your quotes.

Finding the right blogger can also be a challenge. Start off by looking on social media sites like Facebook and Twitter for bloggers talking about your industry. Reach out to them and offer to be a resource. If you're lucky enough that they mention your company, make sure to thank them, leave a comment and a tweet. If they have a Facebook page make sure to "Like" it.

Beyond social media there are a couple of neat tricks using search to find popular bloggers. The first is very easy. Do a search in Google for a keyword associated with your industry or company. Once the search is completed, select "Blogs" from the tools in the top navigation. This will provide results for top blogs focused on those keywords.

One word of caution. Don't bother with any blog on blogspot.com or WordPress.com. Even if they have a large visitor following, the power of their site is shared with the larger domain. Stay clear of any blog that is a subdirectory of a larger domain. For example: mysite.blogspot.com is a subdirectory of the larger BlogSpot website.

The next best way to find popular bloggers is to search Google using certain keyword phrases. In the examples that follow the * is where you would insert your keyword.

"list of * blogs"   Example: "list of law blogs"

"top 100 * blogs"   Example: "top 100 law blogs"

"guest blogger *"   Example: "guest blogger law"

Once you've compiled a list use Mechanical Turk, which is a site where you can hire people per task, to find the owners contact information.

Guest Blogging for Your Site

Once you gain a fair amount of PageRank you'll start to receive requests from bloggers asking if they can post on your site. This is a very exciting moment and you'll want to celebrate. It means your website has gotten noticed. It's possible it was listed in one of the search results we just talked about or it caught the eye of a blogger on Facebook or Twitter.

Either way there are a couple of things you'll want to remember in order to protect yourself from spammers. The number one issue in putting someone else's content onto your site is duplication. First, you need to make sure they haven't stolen content from someone else. Second, you need to check that they haven't already used that content somewhere else.

My favorite application to check for duplicated content is CopyScape. I personally use the Premium service, which checks content for duplication by comparing phrases within the articles I provide against the rest of the Internet. If it finds duplication it shows me each instance with a link. I can then decide if the duplication is acceptable or if I need to hand the article back to the blogger and tell them to fix it.

I know you're probably saying 'wait, when is duplicated content acceptable?'. Good question. There are essentially two times when I will let duplication slide. The first time is the author bio. Yes, it would be great if each time an author wrote an article they also created a new fresh bio but it just doesn't happen. So I live with it. The second time I let it slide is when the duplicated phrase is scientific, mathematic, or legalize. Many times in order to define something correctly you have to use exact phrases that if alerted would lessen the definition of the thing itself.

Other than those two instances all other duplication must be challenged. If your site is caught with the duplicated data, the search engines aren't going to point the finger at the author. They are going to point the finger at you and if your website is seen as a duplication haven, it's going to get knocked down in the rankings.

Where to Find Bloggers to Guest Post

Hold onto your hat because once you start receiving requests for guest blogging opportunities, your website is going to take a major leap forward. Guest blogging is great for the author and provides them with a backlink but you're the real winner here.

The guest post provides your site with additional content, the bloggers audience, and both you and the author willingly promoting it through social media. Additionally, you get to add links to the body of the content and you control the SEO keyword and meta description.

Guest blogging is so hot there are several websites that help you manage the task. I personally use MyBlogGuest, which is a marketplace where authors and site owners meet up. The site is monitored by a dedicated staff that read nearly all the articles submitted. They have some strict guidelines on what they deem acceptable linking. I'll admit I've even had email yelling matches with the owner regarding some of their policies but one of the reasons I like their service is they continue to monitor articles placed from their gallery. If the article is radically modified or the authors backlink is changed, they notify the parties.

When looking through potential articles try to keep the subject relevant to your industry. For example if you run an accounting website, don't post a travel article, unless it clearly relates to accounting. That doesn't mean limiting yourself to only accounting articles. To me accounting is an aspect of business. So an article focused on growing your business is perfectly acceptable. Remember you don't have the ability to modify the article once accepted. It is what it is and if it's not going to help promote your site then you should move on.

It's important to understand that websites like EzineArticles and other article farms are not the same thing as article marketplaces. Article farms are low quality canonicalized content that should be avoided at all cost. If you have articles on an article farm with backlinks pointing to your site, you need to pull them down immediately because they're having a negative effect on your sites PageRank.

Also, consider writing an article on your site to specifically attract interested guest bloggers. Title the article "[insert keyword] Guest Writers/Bloggers Wanted". When an author goes to the search engines looking for blogs accepting articles about that specific topic, your site will be in the rankings.

The article should lay out all your rules and criteria and explain how to submit the article. WordPress allows you to create an open author profile. Writers can input the content of their article and you can review it and decide if you want to schedule it for launch. Make sure the open profile is significantly restricted. That profile should only be able to insert posts. It shouldn't be able to launch the article and certainly should not have access to any other controls on the site.

Take advantage of your sites side navigation and design a self-serving advertisement promoting your interest in guest bloggers. The ad can even link to the article.

How Americans Use Social Media

The chart below says it all. The percentage of Internet users in the United States and Canada dwarfs every other region in the world. So if you're reading this book in Europe, Asia, or anywhere else in the world understand that if your goal is to dominate online you must play in the American market. Everything else pales by comparison.

Internet Users as Percentage of Population

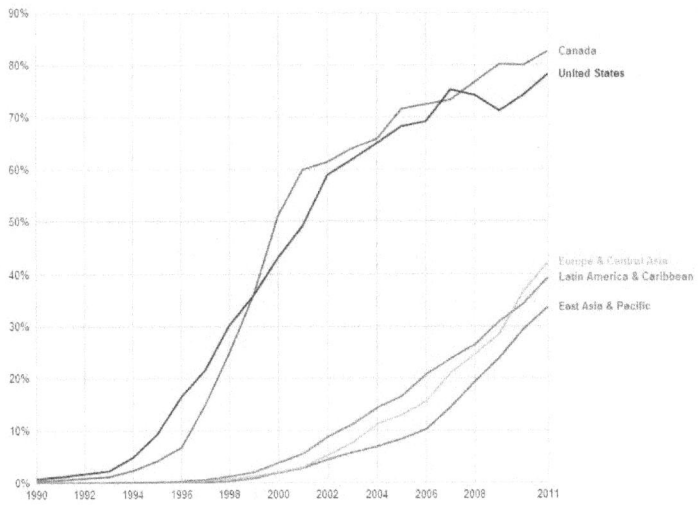

As a business owner with a blog you need to know where Americans are spending their online time. What are they doing and how can you reach them. More than half of Americans over the age of 12 have a profile on at least one social network. Half of them access these networks via mobile device.

Facebook and Twitter are the two largest social media platforms but the competition is ever expanding. Wikipedia has a List of Social Networking

Websites that includes hundreds of sites you've probably never heard of. Beyond the top two you have networks like LinkedIn for professionals; Orkut with a large Brazilian membership; even MySpace is hanging around after getting financing from musicians like Justin Timberlake; but the most surprising is the incredible ramp up of Pinterest that went from zero to an estimated 85 Million Unique Monthly Visitors in 2012.

While Google won't verify their user numbers for Google+, many believe it to be around 40 million. This is significantly lower than Facebook and adoption is only slowing. There is also a huge discrepancy between men at 63% percent usage to women at 37%. A recent survey of activity showed that only 17% were frequent users of the network. Unique visitors also continue to decline, which can explain why out of the top 100 brands only 61% had a Google+ page. However, there does seem to be a correlation between shared content on Facebook, Google+, and Twitter with improved search engine ranking.

Facebook Statistics

With all these networks available the question isn't where to start but how not to get overwhelmed. If you're running a business the majority of your time needs to go into keeping that alive. Maintaining an online presence that is both useful and informative while helping to spread the word about your brand is an arduous task and for small and local businesses it's an uphill battle.

Facebook remains the juggernaut of social media. According to the Nielsen Social Media Report of 2012; Facebook has over a Billion users worldwide. Of those, 58 million Americans check their profile more than once a day. The average age of a Facebook user is 22 and half of all users have had their account for at least three years. In 2012 the average time spent on the site was 27 minutes, which was an increase of 61% year over year.

Hopefully, those numbers have gotten you excited enough to start marketing on Facebook. In a survey to 900 business owners 39% said they plan to advertise on Facebook this year. I'm going to tell you to keep your money in your pocket. You don't need to spend a dime to gain the social media success waiting for you over at Facebook.

The problem with Facebook advertising is that the audience tends to just glaze over the ads. Unless you're advertising a new Facebook App or a hot contest the ads have a very low click through rate.

If you are going to advertiser understand you need a call to action and the ad should lead the viewer to a specific landing page for the sole purpose of getting the visitor to convert quickly. The ads that produce the most results are geo- targeting a specific region. Also, Facebook lets you include a member's photo. Though this is a questionable practice, it is something you can use to your advantage. You can also segment your ad according to specific member interests and likes.

The best way to market yourself on Facebook is to create a fan page. Facebook members 'LIKE' 20 Million fan pages every single day. Once you create your fan page there are some amazing marketing strategies that work well on Facebook. Offering coupons exclusive to your fans is huge. 40% of users said they 'LIKE' a page to get exclusive offers and discounts. Running a contest and awarding a prize for fans can gain you a substantially larger audience. 51% of users post to their wall when signing up for a contest so as to alert their friends. Facebook monitors the success of fan pages. In order to show up prominently in your fans Newsfeed you need to surpass a thousand 'LIKEs'.

As a result of liking brands on Facebook: 77% of those surveyed said they had saved money. 66% saved $20 or more while 17% saved over $100. 46% liked a brand but had no intention of ever buying from them. The reasons they weren't going to buy were: 52% wanted a free item, 46% liked the brand but can't afford the products, 24% liked a brand in order to help a friend.

It's also important to know that 73% of those surveyed have unliked a brand either because the brand posted too often, they stopped liking the brand, or they had a negative customer experience.

Twitter Statistics

Even though Facebook is the most popular it doesn't mean your audience is there. You need to find out which social network your market segment is using and find out how they are using it.

100 million Americans have a Twitter account, which is a significant number less than Facebook. 21 Million users access Twitter at least once a month. 177 Million Tweets are sent every day. Only 16% of those users Tweet via a mobile app but that number has grown year over year almost 185%. Nearly, 65% Tweet directly from Twitter.com on their desktop. Only 24% of all Twitter users check the service several times a day and only 77% of the Top 100 brands have a Twitter account. Significantly, different from Facebook is the average time on site with Twitter less than 4 minutes with a 48% increase year over year. Finally, from the same survey asking 900 businesses about Facebook advertising, only 24% plan to advertise on Twitter.

Buysellads.com believes they have created a profile composite of the person most likely to use Twitter. I'm not sure what scientific method they've employed to figure this out and I certainly neither approve or deny their findings. They believe the penultimate Twitter user is a female Hispanic 20-something who attended college, lives in a city, and makes between $50 and $75K. I think it's a pretty bold composite.

Similar to sharing on Facebook, Twitter has retweeting. Retweeting is the action of re-posting a tweet that a user finds interesting onto their timeline. It's a great way users can share content. If your message is retweeted, it means more people will see it and drive more traffic to the original content. If you retweet other people's Twitter message, you'll increase the amount of content you're providing to your Twitter stream. Retweeting also helps break up the megaphone of messages you're sending out about your services.

You don't want to give your followers the impression your Twitter account is just a bullhorn. Retweeting someone else's message is a great way to breakup that monotony. With Twitter limited to 140 characters, services like Bit.ly shorten URLs allowing you to have room for personalized content. Bit.ly also tracks how many clicks come from the original link, repostings, and the geographical location of the clicks. As you grow, your audience will be looking for you to provide valuable content thus building trust with your audience. Many Twitter users watch who retweets their material and often respond by retweeting your messages.

Infographics Labs conducted a survey to understand why people Retweet. They saw that 92% of those surveyed found the content interesting. 84% had a personal connection with the original Twitter user. 66% retweeted something they found humorous. 21% retweeted something a celebrity tweeted. 32% retweeted because there was an incentive like money or a prize and 26% retweet because there was a request to do so attached to the original tweet.

I feel asking that someone retweets a message is perfectly acceptable. In fact you should ask everyone on all your networks to share, like, and tweet your messages. The best way I've found to ask for content to be shared is to write 'Please Share' at the end of tweets.

Winning with Facebook

The secret to gaining Facebook success is understanding how posts are ranked. At first glance it might seem like the Facebook Newsfeed is just a timeline showing the latest posts from friends. That simply isn't the case. Facebook uses their own algorithm called EdgeRank. The algorithm got its name because Facebook calls every piece of content an "edge". With this algorithm the Newsfeed goes from being a listing of what your friends are saying right now to a ranking of what Facebook deems the most important pieces of edge for the viewer. Essentially, they've moved away from the time stamped Twitter style feed and are exploring the bonds held between people.

EdgeRank looks at three factors: Affinity, Weight, and Time - in order to determine where your post will fall on your followers' Newsfeed.

The EdgeRank Algorithm

$$\sum_{edges\ e} u_e w_e d_e$$

u_e ~ affinity score between viewing user and edge creator

W_e ~ weight for this edge type (create, connect, like, tag, ect.)

d_e ~ time decay factor based on how long ago the edge was created

So how does an individual or business, who's looking to connect with an audience utilize this algorithm in order to improve the chances they'll be at the top of the Newsfeed?

Let's say my undergraduate alma mater was having an event to attract alumni back onto campus. I've already 'LIKED' them and the majority of my Facebook friends are also alumni of that college. However, their Facebook page hasn't had much activity.

So the first thing they should do is start producing content on their Facebook page. Not just random thoughts though. They should begin by posting recent pictures of the campus along with articles from the alumni newspaper and video interviews with professors and students. All of this in order to engage their current fans on Facebook.

The goal is to have the fan base 'LIKE', share, and comment on the content. This improves the individual EdgeRank of each piece but more importantly increases the overall EdgeRank for the page. Thus, giving future content more priority in fans Newsfeeds.

Affinity

The affinity factor is scored based on specific actions taken. Actions including: 'LIKE', comment, tag, and share. Each has a different value to the affinity factor. Liking something only requires a click, while commenting takes more time and effort. Therefore, commenting has a higher value than clicking. Viewing content without taking any action doesn't affect the affinity. Except I believe that if someone's content constantly shows up in your Newsfeed and you take no action it will eventually count against that person and you'll see less and less of them.

Affinity is Facebook's way of trying to provide you with information that you actually care about instead of information that doesn't matter to you. Think of the affinity factor as a proximity meter. Unless you're a celebrity most people have on average 300 Facebook friends. On a daily basis though you're probably just interested in a handful of them. People you don't interact with will be lower on the Newsfeed and you may never see their posts. If they decide to comment on a post, it won't change their rank unless you turn around and comment on their post. This establishes an affinity and changes the EdgeRank for you because you are developing a relationship with them.

The paradox around the affinity factor is that the more times someone is at the top of your Newsfeed the more likely you are to respond, thereby increasing the likelihood they'll be at the top of your Newsfeed again the next time they post an update.

There is an interesting caveat to the affinity paradox. Let's say EdgeRank lists the order of my 300 friends and Mr. 298 is someone who wants to improve their relationship with me so that their updates will appear higher on my Newsfeed. They go to my profile and make a comment on one of my photos. Nothing changes. Why? Because EdgeRank waits till I make a comment back on their profile to consider it an improved relationship. Of course with 300 friends Mr. 298 is going to have to make plenty of comments on my content and I'm going to have to respond in kind. It almost sounds like Facebook is trying to force six degrees of separation but in reality they are just trying not to bombard you with a lot of worthless updates from people you don't really care about.

Weight

The second part of the EdgeRank algorithm is weight. It's the part of the formula that differentiates the types of content into weighted categories. Edge pieces that include videos, photos and links have more importance than just simple comments. So, if being at the top of people's Newsfeed is important you'll want to add some dynamic element aside from just text.

Recency

Recency also known as Time Decay simply means that the more recent posts rank higher on your Newsfeed than older posts. The older a piece of content is the less importance it becomes in the Newsfeed.

This is important for your marketing strategy because you want to post updates when your customers and fans will be reading them. It should be a guide on when to post to your audience. That is why it is important for you to know who your fans are and when they will be online.

College students like to wake up late but they check their Facebook throughout the day. So if you're targeting that segment don't post first thing in the morning but instead do it several times throughout the day. Business people on the other hand might read early in the day and then late in the evening after work.

If you want to get noticed on Facebook as part of your marketing strategy, you are going to have to take time to build a relationship with your followers. Begin by posting relative, informative content on a regular basis. Use visual media to attract attention. Over time as your followers interact with your content your posts will rise in the rankings and you'll be more visible.

Facebook Promoted Fees

All this talk of algorithms might have you thinking you can easily push content to your Facebook fan base. Well there is a slight caveat. In an effort to make money Facebook has implemented a "pay-to-play" promotion fee for messages sent from business pages. If you're not willing to pay to promote your post then only a portion of your fans will see your message in their Newsfeed. Don't fall for Facebook's scheme. Paying for promoted posts only means it's promoted to your fan base. But it's very easy to navigate around this. On your page just remind your fans to hover over the 'LIKE' button and select Get Notifications. As long as this is checked off all your fans will get your messages.

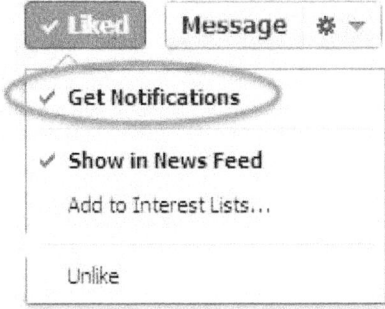

Jonathan Edward Goodman

"You obviously not been reading my Blog."

Jonathan Edward Goodman

WEBSITE DESIGN

Ask ten people what website design is and you'll get ten different answers. Some will incorporate content creation while others will include search engine optimization and even software development. It's not that those people aren't knowledgeable, it's just that the term website designer has become muddied.

I don't blame the client for this mud but instead the freelancers and consultants who overextend themselves to say "me too" when asked if they can do multiple aspects of a project. Everyone wants more business but not at the expense of quality. A designer who also writes code and content is either a genius or fooling themselves and their client.

Web design comes out of graphic design, which was born the instant printing was invented. You could argue this point and say graphic design has been around since man drew on cave walls. I'd disagree and call that illustration. Graphic design and illustration are two different artistic disciplines.

You're probably wondering why I'm making such a fuss over this. It's because as soon as a web designer learns to write code he has boxed himself into what is and isn't capable of being produced on the Internet. He is now working within the constraints of the perceived limitations of the browser.

Instead if a web designer just designs from an artistic viewpoint it becomes the responsibility of the web developer to take that vision and make it a reality. In the past decade, web development has grown to the point that nearly anything is possible. Yet we continue to see the same boxy designs over and over again.

However, when it comes to navigation it's critical that your visitors understand how to move around your site. Your goal is to have them complete an action. That means anything from filling out a form, making a purchase, watching a video, etc. A website is there to engage the visitor and bring them closer to you as a client. If the goal of your site is to have visitors sign up for a newsletter then that must be the main design element. Therefore, it is more important a web designer understands 'call to action' and 'return on investment' more so than how to write code.

Information Architecture

How a site is structured has a strong impact on how it will rank. When designing a site, you want to keep both the user and the search engine in mind.

Information Architecture (IA) is a blend of both art and science. IA is used in several different disciplines but for the purpose of this book I am focusing on its usefulness with organizing the navigation of websites for improved functionality and usability. The building of IA allows the visualization of information taking it from an abstract concept to a concrete framework.

Website IA is drastically more complex than print IA. Print has a continuous theme but each section is separate and distinct from the others. Within a physically bound magazine there can be a theme running through each section that remotely ties into the overall issue but it's hard to cross-pollinate those themes outside of their own sections.

In website IA, elements from within a section might also relate to another section. If the IA is designed correctly the visitor will be invited to continue to the other sections allowing for cross-pollination of content. Additionally, web navigation provides for multiple entry points allowing for content to be found deep within a site. The advantage of a well-designed web IA is it allows the visitor to move from one section to another without backtracking through content that doesn't interest them. It provides a smooth flow of information and the ability to gain access to content needed quickly. In order for the designer to produce an effective IA they must first perform an inventory of all content. During the process of producing an IA the designer might also feel it necessary to create a taxonomy thereby classifying sections of a site and how the visitor progresses.

Web IA can be flat or deep. Flat architecture makes for easier user experience whereas deep IA risks losing the visitor in an exorbitant number of choices. Wireframes are blueprints that show the connectivity between pages of a website. In the wireframe below you'll see how the deep IA hides important elements within the site.

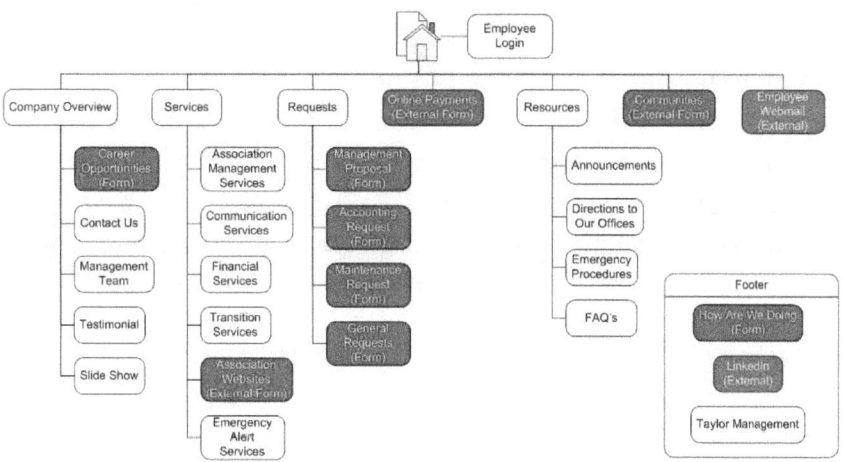

Deep architecture requires the visitor drill down several layers to the content they want. A poorly designed deep architecture will leave the visitor lost and likely to leave before taking an action.

With flat architecture, a visitor can quickly get to the information they want and the action you want them to take from within the first page. It is critical when building out your site that you move through the exercise of creating an IA with your designer. The objective of the exercise is to visually understand how the visitor will move through the site. It is ill advised to skip this phase of site design.

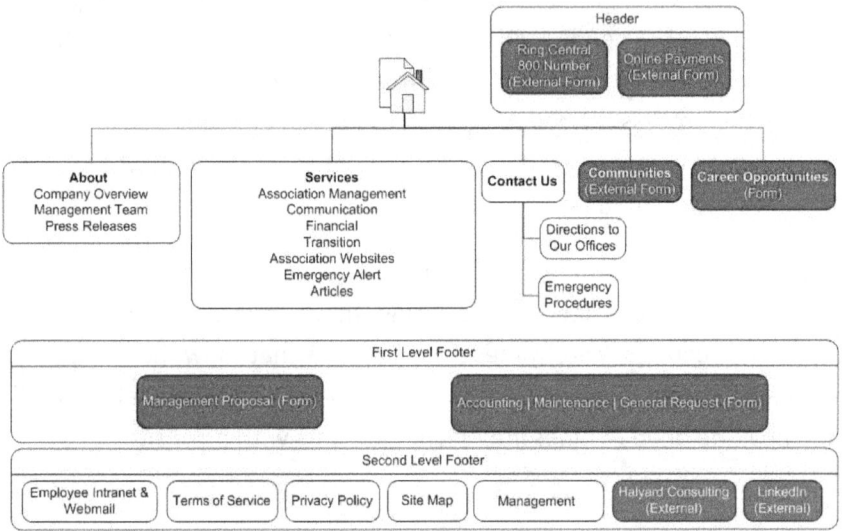

Perfecting the IA also allows you to protect against canonicalization issues. Yes, it's a fancy word that just means duplicated content but the big brain thinkers at Google love to sprinkle SAT words into daily conversation. When a page is canonicalized it means there are copies of the same exact content on multiple pages. Many website owners don't realize that the biggest canonical issue is www versus non-www.

Let's say you have a website called xyzmovers.com and you haven't redirected www.xyzmovers.com to point to xyzmovers.com; then you have a canonical issue. The Googlebot comes in to read data from your site and it reads both xyzmovers.com/index.html and www.xyzmovers.com/index.html. Googlebot thinks there are two different pages and must decide which one to give priority in the rankings. If you redirect one to the other the single primary will gain higher ranking. There are a couple of other major culprits including search results, page numeration, and parameters within .asp pages.

Between a professional designer laying out a good IA and a developer who understands canonical issues you'll be free from any of these headaches.

Subdomains vs Subdirectories

The larger the company and the longer they've been online means the greater potential for self-contained mini-websites circling outside the sphere of the main corporate domain. Somewhere down the chain of command someone eventually suggests consolidation, which then leads to the follow up question: subdomains vs. subdirectories.

Subdirectory = http://xyzmovers.com/blog

Subdomain = http://blog.xyzmovers.com

In the early years of search the subdirectories were seen as separate websites. Optimizers could take advantage of this loophole and gain additional placements in the rankings. With only ten results on each page of a search, dominating several of those spots with subdirectories was a great achievement. However, the overuse of this technique has recently been squashed.

Now when you ask an optimizer which is better subdomains or subdirectories they are generally going to say subdirectories because of the simplicity of the build out. Subdomains require setting up additional DNS information and moving a subdirectory from one server to another is far more complicated. The one advantage to running a subdirectory is if you have different applications running separate elements on your website.

For example if your main website was running WordPress but you had a loan application that ran .ASP, you would place that on a subdirectory instead of attempting to kluge the two applications together. The visitor isn't paying attention to the URLs as you move them throughout the site and won't understand the difference if the look and feel stays the same.

PageRank and domain authority also play into this decision. I'm sure you've heard of trickledown economics. Well this is trickle down PageRank. Essentially, as the primary domain gathers authority through backlinking, you will begin to see improved search ranking. The subdirectory will benefit more than the subdomain. Since subdirectories reside underneath the primary domain they benefit from trickle down PageRank. The subdomain on the other hand has the ability to go out and gather their own domain authority and thus have a different PageRank than the primary domain.

One way to take advantage of this scenario is if you have a company with locations in different states. Segmenting the locations into multiple subdomains will allow you to gather specific location based backlinks for each site.

Examples of Subdomains:

http://newyork.xyzmovers.com

http://newjersey.xyzmovers.com

http://florida.xyzmovers.com

Good Web Design

The New York Times has a specific format for writing their articles and it can be applied just as easily to good web design. The first two paragraphs tell you everything you need to know about what you're reading. It's basically the summary. The middle paragraphs provide further detail beyond the information presented in the first two paragraphs and the final paragraph summarizes the entire article.

Good web design should tell you exactly what the site is about immediately. Then it should guide you through the detailed information and quickly move you to a point where you take an action. The average New York Times reader only reads the first couple of paragraphs and the average site visitor spends less than 27 seconds on each web page.

Good web design is needed in order to move the visitor beyond the average time on page and get them to a point where they complete an action.

A web page needs to be easy to read and easy to navigate without a lot of clutter to confuse the visitor. The site should also have two ways to navigate. One navigation needs to be for the visitor while the other should be for the search engines. I'm not talking about the black hat technique of cloaking, which is when a website redirects search spiders to different content than what humans see on the site. Instead the second navigation needs to be a sitemap.

The original sitemaps were static and made more for the human visitor than the search spiders. They looked similar to IA wireframes. Today, the sitemap link often leads to an .xml file, which is easier for search engines to read. This type of sitemap is beneficial for search engine spiders to understand how your website is set up and if there is additional new content.

Breadcrumbs are an important secondary navigation for humans. Breadcrumbs show the visitor the path they have taken from the homepage to their current page. Breadcrumbs usually reside at the top of a page of content and visually look like this:

Homepage > Category > Content Page.

Each page of content should include internal links within the body of the piece that reference other parts of the site. But be careful about being overly aggressive. Internal linking mixed with external ads should be limited. Placing too many links in the body of an article might have the search engines thinking your site is spammy.

How do you know if your website has good design? Ask several people to complete a specific task on your website. An example of some tasks could be: leaving a comment after reading an article, complete a form or make a purchase. Then ask them this series of questions:

Did the design enhance or detract from completing the task?

Did the design help increase credibility for the site?

Did the design evoke an emotional state?

Did the website provide value?

Would you come back to this site often?

WordPress Design

By now you've probably realized I'm somewhat of a WordPress fanatic. It's a great content management application. It's great for optimizing websites. And yes it's even great for design. Design is particularly fantastic because even if you don't have a stitch of artist skill you can install a beautiful theme from anyone of many design shops.

My only advice for installing themes is to repeat the old phrase "Nothing is ever free". If you find yourself scouring the Internet for a theme to install on WordPress and you come across a site that offers free themes; do yourself a favor and run away. Free themes often times are either poorly written or they include hidden backlinks promoting sites you'd never want to be associated with.

If you are just starting out and can't afford or aren't comfortable managing your website on a server then WordPress.com is great for setting up free domains. There are limitations though and most people aren't happy having a site that's just a subdomain.

Here are a couple of design recommendations once you're ready to starting building out your own site:

Search engines don't read anything **under the copyright** statement so it's pointless putting anything there. In fact if you list a bunch of keywords and link to internal pages Google could consider the site spammy.

In the URL put the name of the blog post before the title of your website (ex. WordPress Design Knowledge Base | Halyard Consulting). In WordPress you can determine how your Permalink structure will look. I personally prefer:

URL/Post Name or URL/Category/Post Name.

Never ever hard code content into a WordPress website. If you are doing this you are missing the point of using WordPress.

Only use Flash if you absolutely must. *Flash is not readable by the search engines.* Yes, there are newer ways to add some information. It just breaks my heart anytime I see an entire homepage made in Flash. If you absolutely must have Flash on the page make sure you have quality content in readable form too.

You can use Flickr Advanced to find *Creative Commons* Images or you can do a Google advanced image search and select the level of licensing rights you need. Creative Commons Images come with a variety of licensing rights. They range from free to use and share non-commercially with no modification; to free to use, share and modify commercially. It really is a fantastic resource just pay attention to the licensing agreements.

Not everything needs to be a *plugin*. WordPress has some great plugins but every time you install another one it's a further drain on your resources. There are some plugins that do such simple things you'd be better off manually doing it yourself.

Accessibility

According to the most recent census there are 54 million Americans with a disability including those that are blind, deaf, and with significant motor dexterity impairment. In this fast pace world we live in the disabled are often times sidestepped and nowhere is it more obvious than on the Internet.

In 1999 the World Wide Web Consortium (W3C) started the Web Accessibility Initiative in order to place focus on the needs of the disabled. Soon after starting the initiative they published the Web Content Accessibility Guidelines WCAG 1.0 and in 2008 updated the document to include technical changes that had occurred over the previous ten years.

Despite the W3C's creation of these guidelines many companies have been slow to implement changes to their websites that would allow for the disabled to gain access. In recent years major companies like Netflix and Target have found themselves the focus of lawsuits centered around the Americans with Disabilities Act. The objective of these lawsuits is twofold. First, it's to highlight a specific company and their inability to comply with federal law. Second, is to send a message to other companies who also are not complying that they need to get in line.

There are assistive technologies available to the disabled like screen reading software that can verbally read out what's on a page. However, having actually tried this software I can tell you it leads to nothing but frustration. Even the best screen readers get caught up blurting out code instead of content. There are screen magnifiers, which enlarge monitor displays for the visually impaired and speech recognition software that accept spoken commands for those with difficulty using a keyboard and a mouse.

It's important though that everyone work together in order to make the Internet more accessible. From developers to browsers the more conscious we are of the needs of those less able the more inclusive the next generation of software can be.

Mobile Websites

According to the <u>Digital Buzz Blog</u> with 4 Billion mobile phones currently in use around the world 1.08 Billion are smartphones. They are expecting by 2014 that mobile Internet usage will take over desktop

Internet usage. Currently, one half of all local searches are performed on mobile devices and 86% are watching television while using the Internet on their mobile devices.

As more people move toward smartphone, tablet, and notebook usage businesses will have to shift their focus from the desktop to the mobile web. It's impossible to view a website designed for a desktop on a mobile device. Most of the time it requires zooming, shifting, and scrolling in order to see the full page and load time is a huge issue.

For a while the answer was to create a mobile subdomain off the main website and market that site to your mobile audience. This meant the nightmare of duplicating nearly everything from the main site onto the mobile site. Not to mention the canonical issues with the search engines. Fortunately, the issue of the mobile website seems to have been resolved through responsive design.

Responsive Design (Fluid Layouts)

On May 25th, 2010, Ethan Marcotte wrote an article called Responsive Web Design and it shook up the web design community. The article highlighted recent technical enhancements that allow websites to determine the differing screen sizes of all viewing displays including tablets, phones, and desktops. The article explained how designers using fluid grids with flexible images could now configure sites for optimal viewing despite variation of display size.

For the visitor, it meant regardless of the device being used they could now gained the best browsing experience. For the companies running responsive websites it meant they no longer had to build out multiple versions of a site just to fit the ever expanding display screens. Ethan Marcotte later went on to write the definitive book on Responsive Design.

With responsive design as a flexible foundation, desktop users can experience a full site with videos, large images, and other content; while mobile users get a simplified version with scaled down images. Mobile devices require simpler navigation and faster load times. These enhanced sites now mold according to the device the visitor is viewing.

Responsive design will allow websites to work on today and tomorrow's devices. It groups similar devices by screen size to create breakpoints. The elastic grid understands the device and platform visitors are viewing and lays out the website accordingly. Media queries determine how images and videos look in the visitor's browser. All of this moves us away from fixed width and goes toward a variable percentage. Designers can now tell images to size down according to the available width and the height will adjust automatically.

Responsive design also allows the content to change based on the size of the screen. The visitor on their desktop may see ten previous posts on the homepage but when on their mobile phone might only see five. There is also an SEO advantage to responsive design. The search engines consider responsive design sites to be mobile ready and rank them higher for searches done on a mobile device.

Content is king but website design is queen and it's become an essential component to getting your site to rank well in the search engines. As more visitors make the switch from desktop to mobile, responsive design is the solution.

ABOUT THE AUTHOR

Jonathan Goodman started his career at the dawn of the Internet age producing ecommerce websites for MicroWarehouse. During the dot.com boom he built the ecommerce site for Earthweb and after the bust he managed the ecommerce site for Suburban Propane.

Jonathan is President of Halyard Consulting, which was founded in 2007 when he recognized the difficulties small businesses had gaining top positions in the search engines. Since then his focus has been to improve the search rankings of businesses with geographically specific customers.

Jonathan earned a Master's Degree in Business Administration from Fairleigh Dickinson University, a Master's Degree in Computer Graphics from the College of New Rochelle, and a Bachelor's Degree in Graphic Design from the Ringling College of Art and Design.

Jonathan has spoken at numerous conferences and conventions running the gamut from higher education symposiums to music industry conferences to WordPress WordCamps.

Jonathan Edward Goodman

ABOUT HALYARD CONSULTING

Halyard Consulting is a New Jersey based Internet Marketing company focused on improving online results for businesses with geographically specific clientele. Gaining top ranking in the search engines is one of the most crucial aspects for Internet success.

Small businesses used to rely solely on traditional marketing strategies like newspapers, commercials, and radio. Today, being visible online is the only true path to success.

Founded in 2007, Halyard Consulting believes that small businesses with limited resources deserve the same opportunities for search engine success as larger companies with powerful budgets.

At Halyard Consulting, our client's greatest return on investment comes from focusing on local market search ranking. Owner, Jonathan Goodman, brings a wealth of knowledge and experience to the marketing challenges of each client. Through his determination and devotion to excellence, he has helped numerous businesses achieve results others could only dream.

When your business is devoted to achieving top search engine ranking, then Halyard Consulting knows the path to get you there.

The Halyard Consulting Equation:
Great Content + A Search Engine Friendly Website + Social Media = Success.

Jonathan Edward Goodman

ADVERTISING

Jonathan Edward Goodman

Get a $50 Rebate

CLICK HERE
http://bit.ly/WpIzED

Making It Click
Powerful Inbound Marketing Training

For professional online marketers who want to stay on top of their game, Making it Click has quickly become an essential resource. Each month members get full-access to actionable, mostly non-boring, video-based marketing training courses.

Lessons feature Danny Dover & Sam Niccolls, authors and industry leaders who've spent over a decade as the hired guns for the world's biggest brands, along with a myriad of online marketing's most respected names.

Making it Click is $176 to join, then $19/mo. However, through July 30th 2013 you can get a $50 rebate simply by signing up, then emailing the promo code **MKG878** to sam@makingitclick.com. All rebate checks will be honored and sent within 30-days of signing up.

Get 10% Off Business Checks

Checks Unlimited™
The Nation's Top Direct-Check Manufacturers

Located in Colorado Springs, Checks Unlimited is set between the towering Rocky Mountains and the expansive Colorado plains. Like the western frontier, they were founded on the solid principles of hard work, integrity, and excellence. From the very beginning, they've kept their sights outward, toward the wide open space of new possibilities.

Established in 1986 as the first major direct mail check printer, Checks Unlimited, was founded to offer an exceptional value on high-quality checks. By maintaining a clear focus on this original objective, the company has evolved and expanded over the years according to customer needs and desires.

When initially introduced, their check line included 13 designs. Today, Checks Unlimited has grown to offer over 70 personal check designs — plus a full line of address labels, checkbook covers, check-related accessories, and a complete line of business checks. Their licensed designs include many of America's favorite icons and characters.

Checks Unlimited is extremely grateful for the loyalty and trust of their Customers!

Get Your Free Copy of The Ultimate Guide to Becoming a Podcaster today!

CLICK HERE
http://bit.ly/WS3VLL

New Media Expo presents
THE ULTIMATE GUIDE TO BECOMING A PODCASTER

The insider knowledge you must know to launch your own podcast and be successful doing it. Have you ever wanted to launch your very own podcast but struggle to understand the steps necessary to get launched and be successful? Fret not, New Media Expo has teamed up with Daniel M.Clark to release the *Ultimate Guide to Becoming a Podcaster*. In it Daniel dives deep into the things you must know to create and launch your podcasting career. The *Ultimate Guide to Becoming a Podcaster* is the latest release in New Media Expo's *Ultimate Guide Series* and teaches you how to:

Choose a topic that works well in podcasting format

Purchase the best equipment for your price range

Record and edit your show like a pro

Upload your show and get listed in directories like iTunes

Promote your podcast to find listeners who will come back week after week

IT'S A MUST READ AND IT'S YOURS FREE.

Check Your Username Availability on 350+ Social Media Sites Free

CLICK HERE
http://bit.ly/Wj4JeO

KnowEm
Secure Your Brand on 350+ Social Media Sites

Knowem.com monitors hundreds of websites for social media identity theft. Knowem.com can instantly monitor brand name, internet identity, or vanity url on over 350 social media websites.

Knowem was developed to assist everyone - from individuals to fortune 500 companies - in discovering where their names, brands, or trademarked terms are available. Knowem not only helps you secure your name across the vast social media landscape but in cases of stolen identity they also show you how to contact each site in order to have the name released and returned to you.

To date the knowem team has helped to reserve over 350,000 profiles and reported over 25,000 issues of squatting and misrepresentation of a brand.

Knowem offers a subscription service for brand protection to ensure you won't have to worry.

DELUXE
FOR BUSINESS

30% Off 1st Order of
Print Marketing Materials

CLICK HERE
http://bit.ly/Y2dclQ

Deluxe for Business
Receive 30% off your 1st order of Print Marketing Materials
Brochures, Business Cards, Postcards, Stationery/Envelopes &
More

All businesses – large and small – are looking for ways to grow. Deluxe works hard to deliver innovative new products and services. As one of their 4 Million-Plus small business customers Deluxe offers thousands of products from forms to retail displays that help you run your business day to day.

Learn more about Deluxe by visiting their website deluxe.com.

Get $50 Discount on Readiris OCR Software

CLICK HERE
http://bit.ly/10FF8vp

**Readiris OCR Software
Converts Your Paper Document into Fully Editable and
Searchable Text Files**

Readiris™ OCR Software is a powerful tool designed to convert all your paper documents, images or PDF into editable and searchable digital text in just a click. Never retype any text again! Readiris™ OCR Software converts your paper, images or PDF files into editable digital text.

Automatically upload your documents to your favorite Cloud hosting service and access it anywhere you are. Import your paper documents from any scanner using the Readiris™ OCR Software scanning wizard.Convert your documents in more than 30 different output formats including Word, Excel, Acrobat, e-Mail, HTML, XML, TXT, XPS and many more!

HootSuite Pro 30 Day Free Trial

CLICK HERE
http://bit.ly/1OQcqgd

HootSuite
Sign up for a Free 30 Day Trial of HootSuite Pro

Manage **unlimited social networks** and profiles under one interface

Schedule Twitter, Facebook, LinkedIn & Google + posts

Track keywords, mentions, and trending topics

Integrated **social analytics** to measure engagement and campaign success

HootSuite is a social media management system for businesses and organizations to collaboratively execute campaigns across multiple social networks from within one secure, web-based dashboard.

Launch marketing campaigns, identify and grow audiences, and distribute targeted messages using the HootSuite unique social media dashboard. Invite multiple collaborators to manage social profiles securely, plus provide custom reports using the comprehensive social analytics tools for measurement.

Free Online Course
Small Business Blueprint
for Online Success

CLICK HERE
http://bit.ly/14xYgPT

Get Your Business Going!!
From Breaking Ground to Going Mobile & Beyond

If you have a website (or even if you don't) you'll be able to dramatically improve your web presence – attracting more leads and customers by acting on this information.

This is a 10-day mp3 mini course and comes with no strings attached!

ACT NOW and also receive the 70-Page Small Business Blueprint for Online Success companion eBook of this popular mini-course as a special bonus.

www.ingramcontent.com/pod-product-compliance
Lightning Source LLC
Chambersburg PA
CBHW071251170526
45165CB00003B/1297

9 781482 074536